The Fumbling Forager's Guide to the Northern Plains

Sabrina Halvorson

There is something infinitely healing in the repeated refrains of nature—the assurance that dawn comes after night, and spring after winter.

— Rachel Carson, Silent Spring

The Fumbling Forager's Guide to the Northern Plains

Sabrina Halvorson

Table of Contents

Introduction

Why 'fumbling'? Because foraging takes humility. There are dangerous plants out there and without careful observation and identification you can end up harvesting something dangerous or even deadly. Humans aren't always great at humility, but I encourage you to embrace it in your relationship with nature. Instead of looking at dandelions as a lowly 'weed', see them as nutritious and medicinal. In fact, I encourage you to reshape your thinking of weeds altogether. A weed is simply any plant that's growing where it's not wanted. Many of those plants have great value and once we realize that, we no longer see 'weeds'. Instead, we see an abundance of nutrition, medicine, and beauty growing all around us. Even in those dandelions popping up in your lawn.

Another part of humility is accepting the guidance of others. It's always a good idea to double and triple check plant identifications, especially if you'll be ingesting the plant in any way. I use an app to double check my identifications and I find it to be extremely useful. I have no affiliation with them, but I encourage you to check out the iNaturalist app. If you do, feel free to look me up under The Fumbling Forager. What I particularly like is that while it helps you identify plants and other organisms using a huge database, it also lets other users double check your identifications and share their input.

If you prefer not to use an app, I do encourage you to find a way that's comfortable for you to double check your identifications. When I'm out foraging, I rely heavily on my husband for help with identification in grasslands. He's a North Dakota native and studied the prairies and grasslands while earning his agriculture-related degree. (He reminds me that it was many years ago, but I remind him sweet grass is sweet grass whether it's 2026 or 1996.) I'm better with flowers and trees than I am with grasses. Grasses all look the same to me.

Along that theme, keep in mind that some plants, even those easy to identify, have close look-alikes that can be very dangerous. I've tried to include tips on how to recognize and "weed out" the impostors.

With all that in mind, head out there and have fun. Be mindful, be careful, and be humble.

Sabrina

Foraging tips

Foraging is a wonderful way to connect with nature, enjoy the outdoors, and gather wild foods and herbs but it also comes with responsibility. The plants you harvest are part of a larger ecosystem, and how you gather them matters. By following a few simple guidelines, you can forage safely, ethically, and sustainably, ensuring these plants are here for future generations of people, pollinators, and wildlife.

1. Avoid Pesticide-Treated Areas

Never harvest plants from areas that may have been sprayed with pesticides, herbicides, or chemical fertilizers. This includes the edges of conventional crop fields, manicured parks, or heavily trafficked roadsides where chemical treatments are common.

2. Harvest Sustainably

As a general rule, you should never take more than one-third of a healthy plant's leaves.

- Taking too many leaves can weaken the plant and reduce its ability to regrow.
- When harvesting roots, always leave plenty of mature plants behind to ensure the population can recover and thrive in future seasons.

3. Positively Identify Plants

Be absolutely certain of plant identification before harvesting or consuming any wild plant. Some edible plants have dangerous look-alikes. Use multiple sources such as photos, field guides, and expert verification if possible.

4. Harvest in Clean Locations

Choose foraging spots away from highways, railroads, industrial areas, or old buildings to avoid plants that may have absorbed heavy metals or toxins from the environment.

5. Harvest Ethically

- Leave enough for wildlife. Many animals and pollinators depend on the same plants you may be gathering.
- Avoid over-harvesting from small or rare plant populations.

6. Know the Laws

Check local, state, and federal regulations. Foraging may be restricted in protected areas like state parks, wildlife refuges, and private property. Here are a few state guidelines. Even within these states, there may be different county regulations. Keep in mind that state laws may change, so check your state before heading out. National parks and Bureau of Land Management land will have different rules.

- **Wisconsin** – Foraging permitted on state land. Only berries, nuts, mushrooms, and ramp bulbs. Only for personal use, no commercial use.
- **Minnesota** – Foraging permitted on state land. Only fruit, berries, and mushrooms. Only for personal use, no commercial use.
- **North Dakota** – Foraging prohibited in state parks, but is allowed in Wildlife Management Areas. Only fruit and berries for personal use.

7. Respect the Plant and the Land

Practice gratitude and mindfulness while foraging. Traditional teachings emphasize harvesting with respect, taking only what you need, and giving thanks to the plants and the land.

Disclaimer
The information in this guide is for educational purposes only and is not intended to diagnose, treat, cure, or prevent any disease. Always consult a qualified healthcare provider before using any wild plant for medicinal purposes, especially if you are pregnant, nursing, on medication, or have a medical condition. Foraging carries inherent risks. Be 100% certain of your plant identification before harvesting or consuming any wild plant.

The Plants

American Plum
Prunus americana

American Plum is a native shrub or tree that produces tart, edible plums. Early spring flowers support pollinators, and the thickets it forms offer excellent shelter for birds and small mammals. The raw fruit is tart, but if you're hungry it will provide nourishment. There's a grove at my favorite foraging spot and I've enjoyed quite a few jars of jam from the fruit.

How to Identify:

- Grows as a large shrub or tree, typically 6 to 20 feet tall
- Often forms dense thickets through spreading suckers
- Leaves are oval, finely serrated, and pointed at the tip

- Clusters of small, fragrant white flowers bloom in early spring before the leaves emerge
- Fruits are round, about 1 inch wide, turning yellow, red, or purplish when ripe in late summer

Look-Alikes to Watch For:
- Other wild plums and cherries — leaves may look similar, but confirm by flower clusters and fruit size
- Young Chokecherry (*Prunus virginiana*) — distinguish by comparing fruit and leaf shape

Additional Notes:
- Fruits are tart raw but excellent for jams, jellies, syrups, or baking
- Fruit is ripe once a yellow/red/purple color
- Handle thickets carefully — branches may have small, sharp spines
- Common along woodland edges, prairies, fencerows, and roadsides
- Important to wildlife — provides food and dense protective cover

Anise Hyssop
Agastache foeniculum

Anise hyssop is a fragrant, upright plant native to the Northern Plains, commonly found in prairies, woodland edges, and pollinator gardens. With its soft purple flower spikes and sweet licorice scent and taste, it's both a medicinal herb and a pollinator favorite. The easiest way to identify anise hyssop is to crush a leaf or flower between your fingers. It should smell strongly of black licorice.

How to Identify:

- Square stems and opposite, toothed leaves with a slight heart shape
- Spikes of small, tubular purple flowers that bloom mid- to late summer
- Leaves emit a strong anise or licorice scent when crushed
- Grows 2 to 4 feet tall in sunny to partly shaded areas

Look-Alikes to Watch For:

- Mint (*Mentha spp.*) — also aromatic with square stems, but has creeping growth and different flower shape
- Giant Hyssop (*Agastache nepetoides*) — similar form but flowers are pale yellow-green and scent is not licorice-like

Additional Notes:

- Traditionally used for colds, fevers, and digestive upset; often brewed as a tea
- Edible leaves and flowers add flavor to teas, salads, or baked goods
- Attracts bees, butterflies, and hummingbirds
- Native to much of the Upper Midwest and a great addition to pollinator gardens

Aronia
Aronia melanocarpa

Aronia, often called Black Chokeberry, is a hardy native shrub that produces small, dark purple fruits rich in antioxidants. These berries are highly valued for their health benefits and have become popular in jams, syrups, and wellness products. I make aronia berry syrup and use it the same way others use elderberry syrup. My recipe is included later in this guide.

How to Identify:
- Deciduous shrub typically 3 to 6 feet tall
- Glossy, oval leaves with finely serrated edges
- Clusters of small, white five-petaled flowers bloom in spring
- Fruits are small, dark purple to black, and appear in late summer to fall

- Grows in thickets, along woodland edges, wetlands, and open fields

Look-Alikes to Watch For:
- Other chokeberry species — confirm by fruit color and leaf shape
- Some wild cherries and plums — distinguish by size, fruit clusters, and growth habit

Additional Notes:
- Berries are very tart and astringent raw but excellent cooked in jams, syrups, or baked goods
- Popular for their high antioxidant content and potential health benefits
- Thrives in a variety of soils, often used in native plant landscaping and erosion control
- Supports birds and pollinators with fruit and spring blooms

Blue Vervain
Verbena hastata

Blue Vervain is a native perennial known for its tall, slender spikes of vibrant blue-purple flowers. It thrives in wet meadows, ditches, and along streams, providing nectar for pollinators and traditional medicinal uses for humans. Historically, Blue Vervain has been used as a calming herb and digestive aid.

How to Identify:
- Erect, branching plant growing 2 to 5 feet tall
- Long, slender flower spikes with small blue-purple flowers blooming from bottom to top
- Opposite, lance-shaped leaves with toothed edges

- Prefers moist soils. Often found near wetlands, stream banks, and damp meadows.

Look-Alikes to Watch For:

- Hoary Vervain (*Verbena stricta*) — similar flowers but prefers dry habitats and has hairier leaves
- Other blue-flowered plants — confirm by flower spike structure and moist habitat

Additional Notes:

- Flowers attract bees, butterflies, and other pollinators
- Historically used in teas for relaxation or mild digestive support — proper identification is essential
- Beautiful addition to native plant gardens and restoration projects

Burdock
Arctium spp.

Burdock is a hardy biennial plant found along roadsides, field edges, and disturbed soils throughout the Northern Plains. Recognized for its large, heart-shaped leaves and burr-covered seed heads that cling to clothing and fur, it is both a useful foraging plant and a cautionary tale about invasive species. The long taproot is edible and has been valued in herbal medicine for centuries.

How to Identify:
- Large, dull green, heart-shaped leaves with a woolly underside
- Thick, hollow, grooved stems that may have reddish tints
- Purple thistle-like flowers in midsummer, followed by round burr seed heads with hooked bracts

- Taproot long, slender, and brown-skinned with white interior
- Common in disturbed soils, ditches, pastures, and vacant lots

Look-Alikes to Watch For:
- Rhubarb (*Rheum rhabarbarum*) — similar large leaves, but leaf stems are edible; burdock's leaves are not eaten raw due to bitterness
- Common Dock (*Rumex spp.*) — smaller leaves and no burr seed heads
- Cocklebur (*Xanthium strumarium*) — burrs are oval and pricklier, leaves are triangular

Additional Notes:
- Traditionally used to support liver and kidney function, as a skin remedy, and to aid digestion

- Burrs inspired the invention of Velcro
- Non-native and can be invasive; harvest

responsibly and avoid spreading seeds

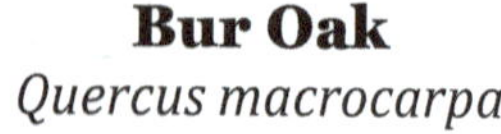

Bur Oak
Quercus macrocarpa

Bur oak is one of the most important trees of the Northern Plains, valued for its large, calorie-dense acorns and long history as a staple food source. This hardy oak thrives along river corridors, prairie edges, and open woodlands, where it can live for centuries. For people relying on the land, bur oak provides one of the most reliable sources of wild carbohydrates and fats available in the region.

How to Identify:
- Large, deeply lobed leaves with rounded lobes and a narrowed "waist" near the middle
- Thick, corky bark with deep ridges and plates on mature trees
- Large acorns with a distinctive fringed or bur-like cap covering much of the nut

- Found in river valleys, floodplains, savannas, prairie edges, and open woods

Look-Alikes to Watch For:
- White Oak (Quercus alba) — similar lobed leaves but generally smaller acorns and less fringed caps
- Swamp White Oak (Quercus bicolor) — leaves less deeply lobed, often with lighter undersides
- Red Oak species — pointed leaf lobes rather than rounded

Additional Notes:
- This entry focuses on bur oak because it is the most abundant in this area. Acorns from other oak species are also edible after proper processing
- Tannin levels vary by species, but all acorns require leaching before use
- Learning to process acorns is more important than identifying oak species with precision

Bur Oak leaf

Catnip
Nepeta cataria

Catnip, a familiar member of the mint family, is a non-native herb that has naturalized widely across the Northern Plains. Known for its effect on cats, it also has a long history of use in herbal teas for humans. Catnip grows easily in disturbed soils and along roadsides.

How to Identify:
- Herbaceous plant growing 1 to 3 feet tall
- Soft, gray-green leaves with scalloped edges and fine hairs
- Small, pale purple or whitish flowers bloom in spikes at the stem tips

- Leaves have a distinct, minty aroma when crushed
- Common in fields, roadsides, ditches, and disturbed soils

Look-Alikes to Watch For:
- Other mints such as Wild Mint (*Mentha arvensis*) — distinguish by leaf shape, fine hairs, and growth habit
- Some deadnettles — confirm by flower structure and strong minty scent

Additional Notes:
- Leaves are traditionally used in herbal teas for relaxation and mild digestive support
- Spreads easily by seed — can be aggressive in garden settings

Cattail
Typha spp.

Cattail is one of the most important survival plants of the Northern Plains, offering food, fiber, and practical materials from a single species. Found wherever shallow water is present, cattails have been used for generations as a dependable source of calories and everyday necessities. Nearly every part of the plant is useful, and established stands return year after year with little pressure from careful harvesting.

How to Identify:
- Tall wetland plant with long, flat, blade-like leaves rising from shallow water or saturated soil

- Thick, upright flowering stalk topped with a dense, cylindrical brown seed head
- Flower head often appears as a two-part structure, with a thinner male portion above the thicker female portion
- Grows in dense stands rather than as individual plants
- Found along marshes, wetlands, lake edges, slow-moving rivers, ditches, and prairie potholes

Look-Alikes to Watch For:
- Iris (Iris spp.) — similar leaf shape but lacks the distinctive cylindrical seed head
- Bur-reed (Sparganium spp.) — rounded seed clusters instead of a solid brown spike
- Sweet Flag (Acorus calamus) — fragrant leaves and different flower structure

Additional Notes:
- Rhizomes are rich in starch and provide an important source of carbohydrates
- Young spring shoots, immature flower spikes, and pollen are all edible
- Leaves can be dried and woven into mats, baskets, and simple roofing
- Seed fluff is useful for insulation and fire starting

Chokecherry
Prunus virginiana

Chokecherry is a native shrub or small tree common across the Northern Plains. While its raw berries are extremely tart, they have been used for generations in jams, syrups, and traditional recipes. Chokecherry thickets also provide vital food and shelter for birds and wildlife.

How to Identify:
- Large shrub or small tree, typically 6 to 20 feet tall
- Oval, finely serrated leaves with pointed tips
- Long, drooping clusters of small white flowers bloom in late spring
- Clusters of small, dark red to purple-black cherries appear in late summer

- Found along woodland edges, prairies, fence lines, and roadsides

Look-Alikes to Watch For:
- Other wild plums, cherries, or Buckthorn — confirm by drooping flower and fruit clusters and leaf shape

Additional Notes:
- Berries are extremely tart raw but used in syrups, jams, jellies, or traditional Indigenous foods
- Leaves, bark, and pits contain compounds that can be toxic — only the properly prepared fruit is edible
- Provides excellent cover and food for birds and wildlife
- Thrives in a variety of soils, often forming dense thickets

Clover, White and Red

Trifolium repens (White Clover)
Trifolium pratense (Red Clover)

You'd think clover would be one of the easiest plants out there to identify, and you'd be right, mostly. While it's pretty easy to know a clover when you see one, there are a few look-alikes out there that are often mistaken for this plentiful plant. Clover flowers are edible, slightly sweet, and good for you. They contain vitamins A, C, and E, as well as calcium, magnesium, potassium, and some protein.

How to Identify:

- Three-parted (trifoliate) leaves, often with a pale chevron mark

- White Clover: Low-growing with creeping stems and small, round white flower heads
- Red Clover: Taller, upright plant with fuzzy stems and larger pink to purplish flower heads
- Found in sunny lawns, meadows, pastures, and disturbed areas from spring through fall

Look-Alikes to Watch For:
- Wood Sorrel (*Oxalis* spp.) — has heart-shaped leaflets and yellow or pink flowers
- Black Medick (*Medicago lupulina*) — trifoliate leaves, small yellow flowers, and dark seed pods
- Hop Clover (*Trifolium dubium*) — smaller plant with yellow flowers, sometimes confused with White Clover

Additional Notes:
- Leaves and flowers are edible raw or cooked and are dried for tea
- Red clover blossoms are traditionally used to support skin health
- Improves soil fertility by fixing nitrogen through its root system

Cutleaf Coneflower
Rudbeckia laciniata

Cutleaf coneflower is a tall, summer-blooming native plant found in moist meadows, woodland edges, and streambanks across the Northern Plains. Its bright yellow flowers with drooping petals and prominent green centers make it easy to recognize and a favorite among pollinators.

How to Identify:

- Upright plant growing 3 to 8 feet tall
- Deeply lobed leaves with a coarse, toothed texture
- Yellow flowers with drooping rays and a raised greenish-yellow center
- Prefers moist soil and partial to full sun; often forms large colonies

Look-Alikes to Watch For:

- Sweet Coneflower (Rudbeckia subtomentosa) — similar yellow blooms but typically shorter, with more rounded leaves and a sweeter fragrance; more common in the Midwest and East than in the Northern Plains.
- Black-eyed Susan (Rudbeckia hirta) — another closely related look-alike with smaller flower heads, rough, hairy leaves, and a darker central cone.
- Sunflowers (*Helianthus spp.*) — broader leaves and thicker stems; flower centers usually darker

Additional Notes:

- Young shoots and leaves were traditionally cooked and eaten, but caution is advised. Consuming raw or in large quantities can lead to gastric problems
- Long history of use in regional herbal traditions
- Can spread vigorously in the right conditions — ideal for wild or naturalized plantings
- Also known as "wild golden glow" or "tall coneflower"

Dandelion
Taraxacum officinale

Dandelion is one of the most widespread and recognizable wild plants in the Northern Plains. Often seen as a lawn weed, this hardy perennial is entirely edible and has a long history of medicinal use. It thrives in disturbed soils and open, sunny areas.

How to Identify:

- Bright yellow flower heads made up of many tiny petals, blooming early spring through fall
- Deeply toothed, hairless leaves growing in a basal rosette
- Hollow, leafless flower stems that exude a milky sap when broken
- Puffball seed heads that disperse in the wind
- Found in lawns, gardens, pastures, roadsides, and other disturbed areas

Look-Alikes to Watch For:

- Cat's Ear (*Hypochaeris radicata*) — similar flowers but with hairy, branched stems and fuzzy leaves
- Hawkweed (*Hieracium* spp.) — yellow flowers with branched stems and leafy growth
- Sow Thistle (*Sonchus* spp.) — taller plants with spiny, lobed leaves and yellow flowers

Additional Notes:

- Entire plant is edible: young leaves, roots, and flowers can be used raw or cooked
- Traditionally used to support digestion, liver function, and as a natural diuretic
- Nutrient-dense, containing vitamins A, C, and K, as well as iron and calcium
- One of the first nectar sources for pollinators in early spring

Echinacea
Echinacea angustifolia, Echinacea purpurea

Echinacea, also known as coneflower, is a striking prairie plant found across the Northern Plains. Valued both ornamentally and medicinally, it's best known for its immune-supporting properties. Echinacea thrives in dry, open prairies and grasslands.

How to Identify:
- Tall, upright plant with rough, hairy stems and narrow to broad leaves depending on species
- Prominent central cone surrounded by drooping pink to purple petals
- Blooms mid to late summer in open prairies and fields
- *E. angustifolia* has narrow leaves and shorter petals; *E. purpurea* is taller with broader leaves and petals

Look-Alikes to Watch For:
- Upright Prairie Coneflower (*Ratibida columnifera*) — yellow petals and elongated central cone
- Black-eyed Susan (*Rudbeckia hirta*) — yellow petals with a dark central disk
- Other purple-flowered garden coneflowers. Check for native species traits like leaf shape and growth habit

Additional Notes:
- E. angustifolia is a native prairie species in much of the Northern Plains and E. purpurea is often garden-cultivated in the region
- Roots and flowers have been traditionally used to support the immune system
- Popular in teas and tinctures for cold and flu support
- Attracts pollinators and supports native prairie ecosystems
- Harvest responsibly. Overharvesting in the wild has reduced native populations in some areas

Elderberry
Sambucus nigra subsp. *canadensis*

Elderberry is a fast-growing shrub found along woodland edges, streambanks, and roadsides throughout the Northern Plains. It produces clusters of white flowers in early summer, followed by small, dark purple berries. Traditionally used for immune support, elderberries must be cooked before eating. Elderberry stems, leaves, and unripe berries contain cyanogenic compounds and should not be consumed.

How to Identify:
- Large, multi-stemmed shrub growing up to 10 feet tall

- Opposite, compound leaves with 5–11 serrated leaflets
- Broad, flat-topped clusters of small white flowers in early to midsummer
- Dark purple to black berries in drooping clusters by late summer
- Found in moist soils near woods, creeks, ditches, and fence lines

Look-Alikes to Watch For:
- Red Elderberry (*Sambucus racemosa*) — red berries and conical flower clusters; less palatable and potentially more toxic
- Water Hemlock (*Cicuta* spp.) — highly toxic; lacks woody stems and produces umbrella-shaped flower clusters
- Pokeweed (*Phytolacca americana*) — tall, herbaceous plant with reddish stems and clustered dark berries on pink stalks

Additional Notes:
- Berries must be cooked before use. Raw berries can cause nausea
- Flowers can be used fresh or dried for tea, syrup, or cordial
- Traditionally used to support the immune system and as a remedy for colds and flu
- Provides valuable food for birds and other wildlife

Golden Alexander
Zizia aurea

Golden Alexander is an early-blooming native plant found in prairies, meadows, and moist woodland edges across the Northern Plains. Its bright yellow flower clusters resemble those of wild parsnip or other members of the carrot family, but it is a safe and beneficial native species.

How to Identify:

- Upright plant growing 1 to 3 feet tall with smooth, branching stems
- Compound leaves with toothed leaflets, sometimes divided further into lobes
- Flat-topped clusters of small, bright yellow flowers blooming in late spring to early summer

- Found in moist prairies, woodland edges, and along streambanks

Look-Alikes to Watch For:
- Goldenrod (Solidago spp.) — similar yellow blooms, but flowers in late summer to fall rather than early summer.
- Wild Parsnip (*Pastinaca sativa*) — taller with grooved stems and more widely spaced leaves; causes skin irritation
- Poison Hemlock (*Conium maculatum*) — white flowers, finely divided leaves, and purple-spotted stems
- Other members of the carrot family — confirm by flower color, bloom time, and leaf shape

Additional Notes:
- One of the earliest native wildflowers to bloom in spring
- Supports native pollinators, including specialist bees
- Often used in native plant gardens
- Host plant for the Black Swallowtail butterfly caterpillar

Goldenrod
Solidago spp.

Goldenrod is a showy, late-summer bloomer found in prairies, fields, and along roadsides throughout the Northern Plains. With tall stems and clusters of bright yellow flowers, it plays a vital role in supporting pollinators. Though often blamed for seasonal allergies, goldenrod pollen is heavy and insect-dispersed, rather than spreading in the wind (which causes most allergic reactions to pollen).

How to Identify:
- Upright growth, often 2 to 5 feet tall, with narrow, lance-shaped leaves
- Bright yellow flower clusters that may appear plume-like, wand-shaped, or flat-topped depending on species
- Blooms late summer into fall

- Found in sunny fields, roadsides, pastures, and open woodland edges

Look-Alikes to Watch For:

- Ragweed (*Ambrosia* spp.) — green, inconspicuous flowers; causes most late-summer allergies
- Yellow Sweet Clover (*Melilotus officinalis*) — smaller flowers on branching stems, with clover-like leaves
- Golden alexander (Zizia aurea) — similar yellow flower clusters, but blooms much earlier in the season (late spring to early summer), while goldenrod flowers in late summer to fall.
- St. John's Wort (*Hypericum perforatum*) — yellow flowers with five petals and bushier growth habit

Additional Notes:

- Traditionally used for urinary tract health and to reduce inflammation
- Attracts bees, butterflies, and other pollinators late in the season
- Used in natural dyeing for shades of yellow and gold
- Numerous species native to the region, all support biodiversity.
- Most *Solidago* species are considered non-invasive, though they are aggressive spreaders

Grapes, Riverbank
Vitis riparia

Riverbank grapes are vigorous native vines found along rivers, woodland edges, and fence lines throughout the Northern Plains. They produce small, tart, dark purple grapes in late summer, beloved by birds and foragers alike. While too sour for most palates when raw, the fruit makes flavorful jelly, syrup, and wine.

How to Identify:

- Woody vine with shaggy bark, often climbing trees or fences using forked tendrils
- Large, heart-shaped leaves with coarse teeth and 3–5 shallow lobes
- Clusters of small, deep purple grapes, usually ¼ to ½ inch wide
- Found in moist woodlands, thickets, and along water edges

Look-Alikes to Watch For:

- Moonseed (Menispermum canadense) — similar vine with bluish fruit; has a single crescent-shaped seed and is toxic
- Virginia Creeper (Parthenocissus quinquefolia) — five-parted compound leaves and small blue berries; also toxic

Additional Notes:

- Fruit is high in antioxidants and pectin, ideal for preserves and wild-fermented drinks
- Young leaves can be used for stuffing, similar to cultivated grape leaves
- A valuable plant for wildlife, as it provides food and shelter for birds and mammals
- Easy to propagate and suitable for wild landscaping projects

A closeup of riverbank grape leaves growing in Minnesota.

Ground Cherry
Physalis spp.

Ground Cherry is a low-growing plant found in sandy soils, open fields, and along roadsides across the Northern Plains. It produces small, yellow flowers that develop into orange fruits enclosed in papery husks, that look like tomatillos. When fully ripe, the fruit is sweet and edible.

How to Identify:
- Sprawling or upright habit, often under 2 feet tall

- Broad, toothed leaves with a slightly fuzzy texture
- Bell-shaped yellow flowers with dark spots near the base
- Round, golden-orange fruit enclosed in a papery husk
- Found in sandy or disturbed soils, fields, and sunny clearings

Look-Alikes to Watch For:
- Horse Nettle (*Solanum carolinense*) — toxic; spiny stems and leaves, no papery husk around fruit
- Nightshade (*Solanum* spp.) — dark berries, not enclosed in husks
- Chinese Lantern (*Physalis alkekengi*) — ornamental species with larger, bright red-orange husks

Additional Notes:
- Only fully ripe fruits are safe to eat. Unripe fruits can be toxic.
- Sweet-tart flavor often compared to pineapple or tomato
- Used in jams, pies, or eaten raw when ripe
- Important food source for wildlife in late summer and fall

Motherwort
Leonurus cardiaca

Motherwort is a tall, hardy member of the mint family found in disturbed soils, field edges, and along fences throughout the Northern Plains. Long valued in traditional herbalism for its calming and heart-supportive properties, it is easy to identify by its square stems and spiky flower whorls.

How to Identify:

- Tall plant, often 2 to 5 feet high, with square stems and opposite leaves
- Lower leaves are deeply lobed and palmate, higher leaves are less lobed
- Small, pale pink to lavender flowers in whorls around the stem, nestled in leaf axils

- Flowers have a tubular shape and bloom from mid to late summer
- Found in disturbed areas, field edges, roadsides, and old homesteads

Look-Alikes to Watch For:
- Hemp Nettle (*Galeopsis* spp.) — similar flowers but with more serrated leaves
- Other mint family plants — confirm by leaf shape, flower arrangement, and height
- Canada Thistle (*Cirsium arvense*) — similar height but with spiny leaves and thistle-like flowers

Additional Notes:
- Traditionally used to support heart and nervous system health
- Bitter leaves are not typically eaten but are used in teas or tinctures
- Attracts pollinators and beneficial insects
- Can spread readily and persist in disturbed soils

Lower leaves of a motherwort plant

Mullein
Verbascum thapsus

Mullein is a unique plant. It is a tall, biennial plant easily recognized by its soft, fuzzy leaves and towering yellow flower spike. Common across the Northern Plains in disturbed soils and sunny areas, it has a long history of use for respiratory support and skin care.

How to Identify:

- First-year plant forms a low rosette of large, velvety gray-green leaves
- Second-year plant sends up a tall flowering stalk, often 4 to 6 feet tall or more
- Yellow, five-petaled flowers bloom in succession along the upper part of the stalk
- Entire plant covered in dense, soft hairs
- Found in roadsides, pastures, open fields, and gravelly or sandy soils

Look-Alikes to Watch For:

- Common Comfrey (*Symphytum officinale*) — also fuzzy, but leaves are narrower and plant has purple flowers
- Lamb's Ear (*Stachys byzantina*) — low-growing and woolly, but does not produce a tall flower spike
- Other tall roadside weeds — confirm by the distinctive soft texture and flower stalk

Additional Notes:

- Leaves and flowers traditionally used in teas or oils for respiratory and skin support
- Dried leaves were once used as torch wicks or tinder
- Flowers attract bees and other pollinators
- Non-native but well established. Can be considered invasive in some instances

First year mullein rosette

Mullein flowers

Plantain

Plantago major (Broadleaf Plantain), *Plantago lanceolata* (Narrowleaf Plantain)

Plantain is a superstar to those of us who are often the target of unrelenting mosquito attacks. This resilient, low-growing plant is found in lawns, trails, and disturbed areas throughout the Northern Plains. Widely used in traditional herbalism, its leaves are known for soothing skin irritations, bites, and minor wounds.

How to Identify:

- Basal rosette of leaves growing close to the ground
- Broadleaf Plantain: wide, oval leaves with prominent parallel veins

- Narrowleaf Plantain: long, lance-shaped leaves with similar veining
- Leafless flower stalks rise from the center, topped with tight clusters of tiny greenish-brown flowers

Look-Alikes to Watch For:
- Common Mullein (*Verbascum thapsus*) — soft, fuzzy leaves and tall flower spike. Young plants can be mistaken for plantain, however mullein does not have parallel veins and plantain does not have fuzzy leaves.
- Dandelion (*Taraxacum officinale*) — similar rosette habit but has toothed leaves and yellow flowers
- Dock (*Rumex* spp.) — larger, more wavy leaves and taller flower stalks

Additional Notes:
- Leaves can be chewed and applied directly to insect bites or scrapes as a poultice
- Traditionally used to support skin, digestion, and respiratory health

Prairie Rose
Rosa arkansana

Prairie Rose is a native wild rose found in prairies, roadsides, and open fields across the Northern Plains. This hardy, low-growing shrub produces fragrant pink blooms and red rose hips, both valued for their beauty and traditional uses.

How to Identify:
- Low, spreading shrub usually 1 to 3 feet tall
- Compound leaves with 5 to 9 serrated leaflets
- Single pink flowers with five petals, blooming in early to midsummer
- Stems have scattered curved thorns
- Rounded red rose hips appear in late summer to fall
- Found in sunny prairies, hillsides, roadsides, and field edges

Look-Alikes to Watch For:
- Other wild roses — distinguish by height, flower size, and leaf shape

- Multiflora Rose (*Rosa multiflora*) — invasive; smaller white flowers in clusters, with fringed stipules
- Blackberry (*Rubus* spp.) — similar thorns and growth but with compound leaves of three and different fruit

Additional Notes:
- Petals and hips are edible. The hips are rich in vitamin C and often used in teas and syrups.
- Traditionally used for immune support and as a gentle astringent
- Attracts pollinators and supports native wildlife
- A resilient prairie species that thrives in dry, open habitats

Prairie rose growing roadside in North Dakota.

Prairie Sage
Artemisia ludoviciana

Prairie Sage, also known as white sagebrush or western mugwort, is a soft, silvery plant found in dry prairies and open areas throughout the Northern Plains. Highly aromatic, it has been traditionally used for ceremonial smudging and medicinal purposes.

How to Identify:

- Silvery-gray leaves covered in fine hairs, giving a soft, woolly texture
- Upright stems, usually 1 to 3 feet tall, often forming dense colonies
- Narrow, lance-shaped leaves that may be deeply lobed or entire
- Small, inconspicuous yellowish flowers in dense spikes, blooming late summer
- Found in dry prairies, hillsides, roadsides, and disturbed areas

Look-Alikes to Watch For:

- Common Sage (*Salvia officinalis*) — garden herb with broader, wrinkled leaves and a different aroma
- Wormwood (*Artemisia absinthium*) — similar appearance but typically taller with more dissected leaves
- Yarrow (*Achillea millefolium*) — also silvery but with fern-like leaves and flat-topped white flower clusters

Additional Notes:
- Has a history of use in certain Indigenous ceremonial traditions
- Historically used to support digestion, respiratory health, and as a topical antiseptic
- Drought-tolerant and important in prairie restoration
- Highly aromatic when crushed — the scent is a key identifying feature.
- Can form extensive colonies through underground rhizomes.

Prairie sage growing in clumps in southeastern North Dakota

Purple Prairie Clover
Dalea purpurea

Purple Prairie Clover is a vibrant native wildflower found in dry prairies and open grasslands across the Northern Plains. With its bright purple flower spikes and delicate foliage, it plays an important role in prairie ecosystems as a nitrogen fixer and pollinator plant.

How to Identify:
- Slender, upright plant 1 to 3 feet tall
- Narrow, divided leaves with 3 to 5 leaflets

- Cylindrical purple flower spikes bloom from the bottom up in mid to late summer
- Deep taproot allows it to thrive in dry, sandy, or rocky soils
- Found in native prairies, dry hillsides, and open grasslands

Look-Alikes to Watch For:
- White Prairie Clover (*Dalea candida*) — similar structure but with white flowers
- Non-native clovers (*Trifolium* spp.) — broader leaves and rounder flower heads
- Leadplant (*Amorpha canescens*) — woody base and denser flower spikes with more leaflets

Additional Notes:
- Flowers attract bees, butterflies, and other native pollinators
- Traditionally used by Indigenous peoples for food, medicine, and tea
- Helps improve soil health by fixing nitrogen
- A key species in prairie restoration and conservation efforts

Purslane
Portulaca oleracea

Purslane is a low-growing, succulent plant commonly found in gardens, sidewalks, and disturbed soils across the Northern Plains. Widely regarded as a nutritious wild edible, it has a slightly tart, lemony flavor and is rich in omega-3 fatty acids. If you can identify purslane, you'll never starve to death (at least in the summer).

How to Identify:

- Sprawling, mat-forming growth with smooth, reddish stems
- Thick, fleshy, paddle-shaped leaves that grow alternately or in clusters
- Tiny yellow flowers with five petals, blooming in full sun
- Found in garden beds, cracks in pavement, disturbed soils, and sunny open areas

Look-Alikes to Watch For:

- Spurge (*Euphorbia* spp.) — also low-growing but with milky white sap and thinner, flatter leaves

- Knotweed (*Polygonum aviculare*) — similar growth habit but with small, papery leaf joints and no fleshy texture
- Young chickweed (*Stellaria media*) — softer leaves and different flower structure

Additional Notes:

- Edible raw or cooked — adds a pleasant crunch and tartness to salads and soups
- High in omega-3s, vitamin A, vitamin C, magnesium, and iron
- Traditionally used to cool inflammation and soothe the digestive tract
- Thrives in hot, dry conditions and disturbed sites

Red Columbine
Aquilegia canadensis

Red Columbine is a delicate and striking wildflower found in woodlands, rocky slopes, and open prairies throughout the Northern Plains. Its nodding red and yellow flowers attract hummingbirds and add vivid color to spring landscapes.

How to Identify:
- Upright plant 1 to 3 feet tall with branching stems
- Fern-like, lobed leaves in a basal rosette and along the stems
- Nodding, bell-shaped red flowers with yellow centers and long backward-pointing spurs

- Blooms in late spring to early summer
- Found in open woods, shaded slopes, prairies, and rocky outcrops

Look-Alikes to Watch For:
- Wild Geranium (*Geranium maculatum*) — similar leaf shape but with pink, five-petaled flowers
- Shooting Star (*Dodecatheon meadia*) — nodding flowers with reflexed petals but no spurs
- Cultivated columbine varieties — similar appearance but often hybridized with varied colors

Additional Notes:
- Flowers attract hummingbirds, bees, and other pollinators
- Leaves and seeds contain toxic compounds — not considered edible
- Traditionally used in small amounts by Indigenous peoples for medicinal and ceremonial purposes
- A native woodland wildflower that thrives in dappled light and well-drained soil
- Though not typically a foraged plant, it is important to the region for its benefits to pollinators

Stinging Nettle
Urtica dioica

If you've ever accidentally stumbled upon stinging nettle, you'll know the importance of being able to identify it. Stinging nettle is a tall, nutrient-rich plant found in moist, disturbed areas throughout the Northern Plains. Aptly named, it's known for the fine hairs on its leaves and stems that cause a stinging sensation. It has a long history of culinary and medicinal use once properly prepared.

How to Identify:
- Upright plant 3 to 6 feet tall with opposite, serrated, heart-shaped leaves
- Covered in fine, stinging hairs that release a mild irritant on contact
- Greenish flowers in drooping clusters along the upper stem
- Prefers rich, moist soils near streams, ditches, and forest edges

Look-Alikes to Watch For:

- Wood Nettle (*Laportea canadensis*) — similar sting, but alternate leaves and a more branched flower structure
- Mint (*Mentha* spp.) — square stems and aromatic leaves, no stinging hairs
- Motherwort (*Leonurus cardiaca*) — taller with lobed leaves and pink flowers in whorls

Additional Notes:

- Leaves must be cooked, dried, or crushed to neutralize the sting before use
- Highly nutritious — rich in iron, calcium, magnesium, and vitamins A and C
- Traditionally used to support joint health, allergies, and as a spring tonic
- Young leaves are best for food and tea — harvest with gloves

Sumac
Rhus spp.

Sumac is a small tree or shrub found along roadsides, woodland edges, and open fields across the Northern Plains. Known for its brilliant red fall color and upright clusters of fuzzy red berries, sumac has both culinary and traditional medicinal uses. Forage the berries while they're still coated in the powder that gives them their bright lemon flavor.

How to Identify:

- Upright shrub or small tree, typically 4 to 15 feet tall
- Pinnately compound leaves with 7 to 31 pointed leaflets
- Cone-shaped clusters of red, fuzzy berries appearing in late summer
- Leaves turn bright red or orange in fall

- Found in dry, sunny locations such as roadsides, slopes, and field edges

Look-Alikes to Watch For:
- Poison Sumac (*Toxicodendron vernix*) — rare in this region; grows in wetlands, has white berries and smooth leaves
- Tree of Heaven (*Ailanthus altissima*) — similar leaves but no fuzzy berries and unpleasant odor when crushed
- Elderberry (*Sambucus* spp.) — also has compound leaves, but produces dark purple berries and white flower clusters

Additional Notes:
- Red berries can be steeped in cold water to make a tart, vitamin C-rich drink
- Traditionally used for food, dye, and medicine
- Only red-berried species should be harvested. Avoid white-berried varieties.

Sumac growing in early autumn at Maplewood State Park in Minnesota.

Wild Bergamot
Monarda fistulosa

Wild Bergamot, also known as bee balm, is a fragrant native mint with showy lavender flowers found in prairies and open woodlands throughout the Northern Plains. It is prized for its beauty, medicinal uses, and ability to attract pollinators.

How to Identify:

- Upright plant 2 to 4 feet tall with square stems and opposite leaves
- Aromatic, lance-shaped leaves with a slightly toothed margin
- Pale purple to lavender flower heads made up of tubular blooms, resembling a shaggy crown
- Blooms mid to late summer in sunny prairies, fields, and open woodland edges

Look-Alikes to Watch For:

- Horsemint (*Monarda punctata*) — similar flowers with a stacked appearance and spotted lower lips
- Other mint family plants — confirm by flower structure and overall size
- Joe-Pye Weed (*Eutrochium* spp.) — taller, with dome-shaped clusters of pinkish flowers

Additional Notes:

- Leaves and flowers traditionally used in teas for colds, congestion, and digestive issues
- Strongly aromatic — sometimes called "prairie oregano"
- Attracts bees, butterflies, and hummingbirds
- A hardy native that thrives in dry, sunny soils

Bergamot growing on a prairie in North Dakota.

Wild Lettuce
Lactuca spp.

Wild lettuce is a tall, upright member of the aster family that commonly appears in disturbed soils, along roadsides, and along fence lines. Young plants form a basal rosette before sending up a branching stem that can reach several feet in height. Leaves are long and irregularly lobed, often with a prominent pale midrib. When the stem or leaves are broken, a milky white sap is released. Small, yellow, dandelion-like flowers appear in loose clusters in mid to late summer.

How to Identify:
- Milky white sap when stems or leaves are broken
- Long, irregularly lobed leaves with a distinct central vein
- Alternate leaf arrangement on an upright, branching stem
- Small yellow flowers resembling dandelions
- Common in open, disturbed areas

Look-Alikes to Watch For:

- Sow Thistle — similar yellow flowers and leaf shape, but leaves are softer and lack the strong milky sap typical of wild lettuce
- Prickly Lettuce — closely related; identified by sharp prickles along the underside of the leaf midrib
- Dandelion — shares yellow flowers and milky sap but remains low-growing and does not develop a tall, branching stem

Additional Notes:

- Milky white latex appears when stems or leaves are broken, a key identifying feature
- Traditionally associated with rest and nighttime comfort in herbal traditions
- Bitterness increases significantly as the plant matures, making young plants easier to work with

- Common in disturbed soils, roadsides, and fence lines, often overlooked as a useful plant

Wild Licorice
Glycyrrhiza lepidota

Wild Licorice is a native legume found in prairies, streambanks, and open woodlands across the Northern Plains. It gets its name from the subtle licorice-like flavor of its roots, which have been used traditionally for food and medicine. Its flowers are typical of a legume: one petal sticking up like a sail, two "wings" on the sides, and a folded bottom portion.

Glycyrrhiza lepidota is listed as a species of "special concern" in Wisconsin, which means its population is facing challenges there. It's much more abundant in Minnesota and North Dakota. Please harvest responsibly.

How to Identify:

- Upright plant 1 to 3 feet tall with compound leaves made up of 7 to 17 oval leaflets
- Small, pale green to purplish clover or pea-like flowers in spike-like clusters

- Distinctive seed pods covered in hooked bristles
- Prefers sandy or loamy soils in open, sunny areas

Look-Alikes to Watch For:
- Groundnut (*Apios americana*) — similar vining habit and compound leaves but with darker flowers
- Sweet Clover (*Melilotus* spp.) — taller, more branched growth with smaller leaves and yellow or white flower spikes
- Other native legumes — confirm by bristly seed pods and root scent

Additional Notes:
- Roots have a mild licorice flavor and were traditionally used by Indigenous peoples
- Not the same species as commercial licorice (*Glycyrrhiza glabra*) but shares similar compounds
- Supports nitrogen fixation and prairie soil health
- Bristly seed pods can cling to clothing and animal fur

Wild licorice with brown seed pods in North Dakota

Wood Sorrel
Oxalis spp.

Wood Sorrel is a delicate, clover-like plant found in shaded forests, lawns, and open meadows throughout the Northern Plains. Its tangy, lemon-flavored leaves make it a favorite wild nibble, though it should be consumed in moderation due to oxalic acid content.

How to Identify:

- Low-growing plant with three heart-shaped leaflets per stem
- Leaves fold downward at night or during intense sun

- Small, five-petaled flowers, usually yellow, pink, or white depending on species
- Found in shady woods, garden beds, lawns, and along trails

Look-Alikes to Watch For:
- Clover (*Trifolium* spp.) — rounder leaflets with chevron markings and different flower structure
- Black Medick (*Medicago lupulina*) — similar trifoliate leaves but with small yellow flower clusters and kidney-shaped leaflets
- Violet (*Viola* spp.) — similar ground habit but with broader leaves and distinct flowers

Additional Notes:
- Leaves, flowers, and seed pods are edible and have a tart, lemony flavor
- Traditionally used to quench thirst and as a mild digestive aid
- Contains oxalic acid, which is safe in small amounts but not for regular consumption by those with kidney issues
- Often among the first wild edibles to appear in spring
- Leaves fold closed in low light, rain, or when touched — a helpful identifying feature
- More tender and flavorful in spring and early summer than later in the season

Yarrow
Achillea millefolium

Yarrow is a hardy, aromatic plant found in grasslands, roadsides, and open woods throughout the Northern Plains. Known for its finely divided leaves and clustered white flowers, yarrow has been used for centuries in herbal medicine, particularly for wound care.

How to Identify:

- Upright plant 1 to 3 feet tall with feathery, fern-like leaves
- Flat-topped clusters made up of many tiny white (sometimes pink) flowers, each with small ray petals
- Leaves are aromatic and deeply divided into many fine segments
- Blooms from early to late summer in dry, sunny areas

Look-Alikes to Watch For:

- Queen Anne's Lace (*Daucus carota*) — similar flower shape but with finely divided leaves more like carrot tops
- Poison Hemlock (*Conium maculatum*) — highly toxic; smooth, hairless stems with purple blotches and a foul odor
- Wild Carrot — also resembles yarrow but has a hairy stem and central purple flower dot
- Tansy (*Tanacetum vulgare*) — yellow button-like flowers and more coarse, bitter-scented leaves

Additional Notes:

- Traditionally used to stop bleeding, reduce inflammation, and support digestion
- Leaves and flowers can be made into teas, tinctures, or poultices
- Attracts pollinators and beneficial insects
- Hardy and drought-tolerant — thrives in a wide range of habitats

Plant Type Index

Aquatic Plants
Cattail

Forbs & Wildflowers
Anise Hyssop
Blue Vervain
Burdock
Catnip
Clover, White and Red
Cutleaf Coneflower
Dandelion
Echinacea
Golden Alexander
Goldenrod
Ground Cherry
Motherwort
Mullein
Plantain
Prairie Rose
Prairie Sage
Purple Prairie Clover
Purslane
Red Columbine
Stinging Nettle

Wild Bergamot
Wild Lettuce
Wild Licorice
Wood Sorrel
Yarrow

Trees & Shrubs
American Plum
Aronia
Bur Oak
Chokecherry
Elderberry
Sumac

Vines
Grapes, Riverbank

Recipes and Remedies

I love finding new ways to enjoy my foraged harvest, and I also love experimenting in the kitchen. From herbal breads to soothing skin salves to colorful cookies, there are innumerous ways we can incorporate these wild plants into our lives.

I'm sharing some of my favorite recipes that I've created with plants featured in this guide. I've tried to keep the recipes on the easier side, and I strongly encourage you to make them your own by changing out one or two ingredients.

I've found that food is also a great way to get your loved ones involved in your foraging. Whether it's baking goldenrod cookies with your sweetheart or creating beautiful tins of plantain salve for gifts, creating from foraging gives us the chance to share our passion and introduce others to the bounty around us.

Enjoy these starter recipes and perhaps jump into creating your own!

Aronia Berry Syrup

A deep purple, antioxidant-rich syrup that's easy to make and endlessly useful. I use it to sweeten my teas, but you can also drizzle it over pancakes or simply take it by the spoonful as a daily boost. Can substitute with elderberries.

Ingredients
- 1 cup aronia berries (fresh or frozen)
- 1 cup water
- ¾ cup raw or pasteurized honey
- 2 tablespoons lemon juice (bottled preferred for acidity consistency)

Directions
Simmer: Combine berries and water in a saucepan. Simmer 15–20 minutes, mashing gently to release juices.
Strain: Cool slightly, then strain and discard solids.
Cool: Allow liquid to cool to about 110 °F (warm to the touch).
Mix: Stir in honey and lemon juice until fully dissolved.
Store: Pour into a sterilized jar. Label and refrigerate.

Shelf Life
Keeps in the refrigerator for 3 to 6 months. Freeze for up to a year.

Northern Nettle Berry Tea

No, nettles don't have berries. I've named it nettle berry to include the rose hips and aronia berry syrup. Nettle can be drying for some people, and the marshmallow root helps to counteract that dryness. You can find marshmallow root at herbal tea stores, if you can't forage it near you. Nourishing and refreshing, it's perfect over ice on warm days but I also drink it warm during the winter.

Ingredients
- 1 tablespoon dried nettle leaf
- 1 tablespoon dried rose hips
- 1 tablespoon dried marshmallow root
- 2 cups water
- 2 teaspoons aronia berry syrup (or to taste)

Directions
Simmer: In a small pot, combine rose hips and marshmallow root with water. Simmer for 15–20 minutes.

Steep: Remove from heat, add nettle, cover, and steep for another 15–20 minutes.

Strain: Strain well, then add in aronia berry syrup.

Cattail Rhizome Starch

Cattail rhizomes are one of the most important sources of wild carbohydrates in the Northern Plains. When processed, they yield a fine starch that can be used much like flour in simple cooking. This method takes time, but the result is a shelf-stable ingredient that can help sustain people when other food sources are limited.

Ingredients:
- Fresh cattail rhizomes
- Clean water

Instructions:
Harvest rhizomes in fall or early spring from clean, unpolluted water. Scrub thoroughly to remove mud and outer fibers.
Chop or crush the rhizomes into small pieces.
Place pieces in a bowl and cover with water. Work the mixture by hand to release the starch into the water.
Strain out the fibrous material and set the starchy water aside.
Allow the water to settle. The starch will sink to the bottom.
Carefully pour off the clear water, leaving the starch behind.

Spread the starch in a thin layer and allow it to dry completely.
Store in a sealed container and use as a flour substitute or thickener.

Notes:

• Cattail starch works best when blended with other flours.
• Always harvest from clean water sources, as cattails readily absorb contaminants.

What to Expect:

• Cattail flour is pale cream to light beige in color and is often slightly coarser than store-bought flour
• It behaves more like cornstarch than wheat flour and does not rise or form elastic dough
• When mixed with water, it thickens quickly and has a smooth, starchy texture
• Best used as a thickener or blended with other flours rather than used on its own
• Flavor is mild and neutral, taking on the taste of whatever it is cooked with

Elderberry Muffins

These muffins bake up a deep, lovely purple, with elderberries that soften while keeping a slight crunch from their tiny seeds. They are lightly sweet, hearty without being heavy, and a simple way to bring a wild fruit into everyday baking.

Ingredients
- 2 cups all-purpose flour
- 1 teaspoon baking powder
- 1/2 teaspoon baking soda
- 1/2 teaspoon salt
- 1/2 teaspoon cinnamon (optional)
- 1/2 cup sugar
- 1/2 cup butter, melted
- 2 large eggs
- 1 cup plain yogurt or sour cream
- 1 teaspoon vanilla extract
- 1 1/2 cups fresh or frozen elderberries

Directions
Mix dry: Whisk flour, baking powder, baking soda, salt, and cinnamon in a large bowl.
Mix wet: In a separate bowl, whisk sugar, melted butter, eggs, yogurt, and vanilla until smooth.
Combine: Add wet ingredients to dry ingredients and stir

just until combined.

Fold: Gently fold in elderberries.

Bake: Divide batter evenly among 12 muffin cups. Bake at 375 degrees for 18–22 minutes, until tops spring back lightly.

Cool: Let muffins cool in the pan for 5 minutes, then transfer to a rack.

Wild Plum Jam

This simple, sweet-tart jam highlights the bright flavor of wild plums without added pectin. It's a beautiful way to preserve a seasonal abundance. I strain the skins out for a smooth texture, but you can leave them in if you prefer.

Ingredients
- 3 pounds wild plums (washed and halved)
- 1 cup granulated sugar
- 2 tablespoons bottled lemon juice

Directions
Simmer: Place plums in a large pot with just enough water to prevent sticking. Simmer over medium heat until soft, about 15–20 minutes.
Strain: Press through a fine mesh strainer or food mill to remove pits and skins.
Cook: Return the pulp to the pot. Add sugar and lemon juice. Simmer over low heat, stirring often, until thickened to your liking—about 30–40 minutes.
Store: Pour into clean jars, label, and refrigerate.

Shelf Life
Keeps in the refrigerator for up to 1 month or freeze for longer storage.

Plantain Salve

This soothing salve is a go-to for bug bites, minor cuts, and skin irritation. Made from the leaves of the common plantain plant (*Plantago spp.*), it's wonderfully effective. Plantain has a compound called *aucubin*. It's an anti-inflammatory and antimicrobial agent that helps reduce swelling, draw out toxins, and calm the skin. This is the remedy I make most often. It's a few steps to get to the finished product, and the oil can take a while to infuse, so it's not quick but it's definitely worth it.

Ingredients
- Dried plantain leaves
- Olive oil (enough to fully cover the leaves)
- Beeswax (about 1 ounce per 4 ounces infused oil, for a creamy texture)
- Optional: vitamin E oil (for extended shelf life)

Directions
Infuse the oil
Choose one of the following methods:
- *Traditional infusion*: Place dried plantain leaves in a clean, dry jar and cover completely with olive oil, making sure the plant material is fully submerged. Cap tightly and store the jar in a cool, dark place for 4–6 weeks,

shaking gently every few days to redistribute the herbs.
• *Quick heat infusion*: Combine leaves and oil in a double boiler or heat-safe bowl over simmering water. Warm gently for 1–2 hours, keeping the temperature low.

Strain

Once infused, strain out the plant material using a fine mesh strainer or cheesecloth.

Make the salve

Measure your infused oil. For every 3 ounces of oil, add about 1 ounce of beeswax. Melt together gently over low heat until fully combined. Optional: Add a few drops of vitamin E oil just before pouring.

Pour and cool

Pour the warm mixture into clean tins or jars. Let cool completely before sealing and labeling.

Shelf Life

Keeps for up to 1 year when stored in a cool, dry place.

Dandelion Flower Fritters

These golden fritters are a fun, nostalgic way to enjoy spring's first burst of blooms. Dandelion flowers have a mild, slightly sweet flavor and a satisfying texture when battered and crisped. Try them warm with a drizzle of honey or dusted with powdered sugar.

Ingredients
• About 1–2 cups fresh dandelion flower heads (just the yellow heads, green base trimmed)
• ½ cup all-purpose flour
• 1 tablespoon sugar (optional, for sweet version)
• 1 egg
• ½ cup milk or milk alternative
• Pinch of salt
• Butter or oil for frying (such as sunflower or avocado oil)

Directions
Harvest: Pick dandelion flowers on a dry, sunny day. Remove green bases and rinse flowers gently. Let dry on a towel.
Make the batter: In a small bowl, whisk together flour, sugar (if using), salt, egg, and milk until smooth. The batter should be thick enough to coat a flower.

Dip and fry: Heat a skillet over medium heat and add a small amount of oil or butter. Dip each flower head into the batter and place face-down in the hot pan. Fry until golden brown, about 1–2 minutes per side.

Serve: Enjoy warm. For sweet fritters, drizzle with honey or sprinkle with powdered sugar. For savory, try with herbed salt or a side of sour cream.

Tips

- Best served fresh—crisp on the outside, tender inside.
- These pair well with herbal tea or fresh spring greens.
- Use only flowers from unsprayed areas.

Clover Lemonade

A floral twist on a summertime classic. This lemonade uses clover blossoms for a light, gently sweet flavor that pairs beautifully with fresh lemon and honey. It's refreshing, pretty, and easy to make from foraged blooms.

Ingredients
- 1 cup fresh clover blossoms (red or white), or ½ cup dried
- 2 cups hot water
- 2–3 tablespoons raw honey (or to taste)
- ½ cup lemon juice (fresh or bottled)
- 2 cups cold water
- Optional: lemon slices or mint sprigs for garnish

Directions
Infuse: Place clover blossoms in a heat-safe jar or bowl. Pour 2 cups hot (not boiling) water over the blossoms. Cover and steep for 20–30 minutes.

Strain: Remove the flowers and stir in honey while the tea is still warm. Let cool.

Mix: In a pitcher, combine the clover tea, lemon juice, and cold water. Stir well and taste. Adjust sweetness or lemon as desired.

Serve: Pour over ice and garnish with fresh lemon slices or mint, if using.

Tips
• Use only blossoms from unsprayed areas.
• This recipe makes about 4 servings and can easily be doubled.
• Red clover gives a slightly deeper flavor and a hint of color; white clover is lighter and more delicate.

Wild Bergamot Tea

Fragrant and calming, this prairie native makes a bold herbal tea with a flavor reminiscent of oregano and Earl Grey.

Ingredients
• 1 tablespoon dried wild bergamot leaves and/or flowers
• 1½ cups hot water
• Optional: honey or lemon, to taste

Directions
Steep: Place wild bergamot in a heat-safe jar or mug. Pour hot (not boiling) water over the herbs. Cover and steep for 10–15 minutes.
Strain: Strain out the herbs and sweeten with honey or a squeeze of lemon, if desired.
Serve: Sip warm, or chill and serve over ice for a refreshing summer drink.

Tips
• Use dried leaves, flowers, or a mix—flowers will give a softer, more floral flavor.
• This tea pairs well with mint, lemon balm, or elderflower.
• Harvest only from unsprayed, healthy plants and dry thoroughly before storing.

Elderberry Baked Apples

A simple, old-fashioned dessert with a wild twist. These baked apples are filled with oats, honey, and a splash of elderberry syrup or dried berries for a gently sweet, richly colored dish that feels like fall in every bite.

Ingredients
- 4 medium apples (firm varieties like Honeycrisp or Haralson)
- ¼ cup rolled oats
- 2 tablespoons chopped nuts (optional: walnuts or pecans)
- 2 tablespoons honey (plus more for drizzling)
- 2 tablespoons elderberry syrup *or* 1 tablespoon dried elderberries
- ½ teaspoon cinnamon
- Pinch of salt
- ½ cup water

Directions
Prep the apples: Preheat oven to 350°F. Core apples, leaving the bottom intact to hold the filling. Place in a small baking dish.
Make the filling: In a bowl, mix oats, nuts (if using), honey, elderberry syrup or berries, cinnamon, and salt.
Fill and bake: Spoon the mixture into the apples. Pour water into the base of the dish to prevent sticking. Cover loosely with foil.
Bake: Bake 30–40 minutes, or until apples are tender but

still hold their shape.
Serve: Let cool slightly. Drizzle with a little extra honey if desired. Best served warm, with yogurt or ice cream.

Tips
• If using dried elderberries, soak them in a bit of warm water before mixing.
• Try adding a splash of lemon juice or zest for brightness.
• This recipe can be doubled or halved easily.

Possible Substitutes
• Wild apples or crabapples in place of store-bought apples
• Aronia berry syrup in place of elderberry syrup

Goldenrod Honey Cookies

Goldenrod adds a soft, earthy-floral note to these lightly spiced cookies. They're simple to make and taste like a warm late-summer day.

Ingredients
- ½ cup butter, softened
- ½ cup honey (wildflower or goldenrod honey, if available)
- ¼ cup brown sugar
- 1 egg
- 1 teaspoon vanilla extract
- 1¼ cups all-purpose flour
- ¼ teaspoon baking soda
- ¼ teaspoon salt
- ½ teaspoon cinnamon (optional, but lovely)
- 1–2 tablespoons dried goldenrod flowers, crushed or sifted (remove stems)

Directions
Prep: Preheat oven to 350°F. Line a baking sheet with parchment paper.

Mix wet ingredients: In a bowl, cream together butter, honey, and brown sugar until smooth and light. Beat in the egg and vanilla.

Mix dry ingredients: In another bowl, whisk together

flour, baking soda, salt, cinnamon, and goldenrod flowers.

Combine: Add dry ingredients to wet and stir until fully combined. Dough will be soft.

Bake: Drop by rounded spoonfuls onto baking sheet, spaced apart. Bake 9–11 minutes or until the edges are just golden. Let cool on a rack.

Tips

• Gently toasting the goldenrod in a dry pan can bring out a nuttier, stronger flavor.

• These cookies are soft and fragrant. For a crisper cookie, flatten slightly before baking.

• Use freshly dried goldenrod for best flavor—flowers should still smell lightly spicy or herbal.

Yarrow Foot Soak

Yarrow has long been used in folk herbalism for its skin-soothing, antimicrobial, and anti-inflammatory properties. This foot soak is a simple way to rest tired feet, ease minor skin irritation, and enjoy the earthy, slightly spicy scent of this beautiful wild herb.

Ingredients
- ¼ cup dried yarrow (flowers and/or leaves)
- 4 cups hot water
- Optional: a handful of Epsom salts or a few drops of essential oil (such as lavender or tea tree)

Directions
Steep: Place dried yarrow in a heat-safe bowl or basin. Pour hot (not boiling) water over the herbs and cover. Let steep for 15–20 minutes.
Strain: Strain out the plant material if desired, or leave it in for a more rustic soak.
Soak: Pour the infusion into a foot basin with enough warm water to comfortably soak your feet. Add Epsom salts or essential oil if using. Soak for 15–30 minutes.

Tips
- Yarrow is traditionally used to support skin healing and help ease inflammation.
- Great after a long day on your feet or time spent

outdoors.
• Always harvest yarrow from clean, unsprayed places
and dry thoroughly before storing.

Other Herbs to Add or Substitute
• **Mint** – cooling and invigorating
• **Sage** – aromatic and cleansing
• **Rosemary** – warming and stimulating
• **Lavender** – calming and fragrant
• **Calendula** – gentle and skin-supportive
• **Pine needles** – resinous and refreshing

Mix and match based on the season, your needs, or what
you have on hand.

Chokecherry BBQ Sauce

Chokecherries give this rich, tangy sauce a deep Northern Plains flavor that pairs beautifully with bison, venison, pork, duck, beef, or grilled chicken. This small-batch recipe makes about two cups of sauce.

Ingredients

2 cups chokecherry berries (washed)
1 cup water
1/2 cup apple cider vinegar
1/2 cup brown sugar (or to taste)
1/4 cup chopped onion
1 clove garlic, minced
1 tablespoon tomato paste
1/2 teaspoon smoked paprika
1/4 teaspoon black pepper
1/4 teaspoon salt
Pinch cayenne (optional)

Directions

Cook fruit: In a saucepan, combine chokecherries and water. Simmer 15 minutes, mashing berries as they soften.

Strain: Pass mixture through a fine sieve to remove seeds and skins, pressing to extract as much pulp as possible.

Make sauce: Return pulp to the pan. Add vinegar, sugar, onion, garlic, tomato paste, smoked paprika, pepper, salt, and cayenne.

Simmer: Cook 15–20 minutes, stirring often, until thickened.

Finish: Taste and adjust seasoning. Store in the fridge for up to 2 weeks or freeze for longer storage.

Tips

• For a smoother sauce, blend after cooking.

• This recipe makes about 2 cups. Double it for canning or larger harvests.

• Works well as a glaze for roasting or grilling in the final minutes of cooking.

Field Notes

Use these pages to record what you find, when and where you found it, and any observations you want to remember. Writing things down helps build a deeper understanding of the plants—how they change with the seasons, where they prefer to grow, and how they interact with the surrounding landscape.

There's no need to be scientific or precise. Note the weather, the scent of the leaves, the color of the stems, or simply how the plant caught your attention. Over time, these field notes become a personal record of learning and discovery.

You may also choose to collect and press a few leaves for reference. It's always nice to have an actual leaf to look at.

My Field Notes

DATE: _________**LOCATION:** _______________________________

PLANT NAME: ____

HABITAT + CONDITIONS:
☐ Prairie   ☐ Woodland edge   ☐ Wetland
☐ Roadside
☐ Dry   ☐ Moist   ☐ Sunny   ☐ Shady

OBSERVATIONS:
(leaves, flowers, scent, growth pattern)

____

____

____

STAGE:
☐ Early growth   ☐ Flowering   ☐ Fruiting   ☐ Going
to seed

HARVESTED? ☐ Yes   ☐ No

USED IN: ________________

NOTES:

My Field Notes

DATE: _________**LOCATION:** _______________________________

PLANT NAME: ____

HABITAT + CONDITIONS:
☐ Prairie   ☐ Woodland edge   ☐ Wetland
☐ Roadside
☐ Dry   ☐ Moist   ☐ Sunny   ☐ Shady

OBSERVATIONS:
(leaves, flowers, scent, growth pattern)

____

____

____

STAGE:
☐ Early growth   ☐ Flowering   ☐ Fruiting   ☐ Going
to seed

HARVESTED? ☐ Yes   ☐ No

USED IN: _________________

NOTES:

My Field Notes

DATE: _________**LOCATION:** _______________________________

PLANT NAME: _______________________________________

HABITAT + CONDITIONS:
☐ Prairie   ☐ Woodland edge   ☐ Wetland
☐ Roadside
☐ Dry   ☐ Moist   ☐ Sunny   ☐ Shady

OBSERVATIONS:
(leaves, flowers, scent, growth pattern)

____

____

____

STAGE:
☐ Early growth   ☐ Flowering   ☐ Fruiting   ☐ Going
to seed

HARVESTED? ☐ Yes   ☐ No

USED IN: ____________________

NOTES:

My Field Notes

DATE: _________ **LOCATION:** _______________________

PLANT NAME: _________________________________

HABITAT + CONDITIONS:
☐ Prairie   ☐ Woodland edge   ☐ Wetland
☐ Roadside
☐ Dry   ☐ Moist   ☐ Sunny   ☐ Shady

OBSERVATIONS:
(leaves, flowers, scent, growth pattern)

____

____

____

STAGE:
☐ Early growth   ☐ Flowering   ☐ Fruiting   ☐ Going
to seed

HARVESTED? ☐ Yes   ☐ No

USED IN: _______________

NOTES:

My Field Notes

DATE: __________**LOCATION:** _________________________________

PLANT NAME: ____

HABITAT + CONDITIONS:
☐ Prairie   ☐ Woodland edge   ☐ Wetland
☐ Roadside
☐ Dry   ☐ Moist   ☐ Sunny   ☐ Shady

OBSERVATIONS:
(leaves, flowers, scent, growth pattern)

____

____

____

STAGE:
☐ Early growth   ☐ Flowering   ☐ Fruiting   ☐ Going
to seed

HARVESTED? ☐ Yes   ☐ No

USED IN: _________________

NOTES:

My Field Notes

DATE: _________ **LOCATION:** ______________________

PLANT NAME: _______________________________

HABITAT + CONDITIONS:
☐ Prairie   ☐ Woodland edge   ☐ Wetland
☐ Roadside
☐ Dry   ☐ Moist   ☐ Sunny   ☐ Shady

OBSERVATIONS:
(leaves, flowers, scent, growth pattern)

____

____

____

STAGE:
☐ Early growth   ☐ Flowering   ☐ Fruiting   ☐ Going
to seed

HARVESTED? ☐ Yes   ☐ No

USED IN: ________________

NOTES:

My Field Notes

DATE: _________**LOCATION:** __________________________

PLANT NAME: ___________________________________

HABITAT + CONDITIONS:
☐ Prairie ☐ Woodland edge ☐ Wetland
☐ Roadside
☐ Dry ☐ Moist ☐ Sunny ☐ Shady

OBSERVATIONS:
(leaves, flowers, scent, growth pattern)

____

____

____

STAGE:
☐ Early growth ☐ Flowering ☐ Fruiting ☐ Going
to seed

HARVESTED? ☐ Yes ☐ No

USED IN: _________________

NOTES:

My Field Notes

DATE: ___________ **LOCATION:** _________________________

PLANT NAME: _____________________________________

HABITAT + CONDITIONS:
☐ Prairie   ☐ Woodland edge   ☐ Wetland
☐ Roadside
☐ Dry   ☐ Moist   ☐ Sunny   ☐ Shady

OBSERVATIONS:
(leaves, flowers, scent, growth pattern)

____

____

____

STAGE:
☐ Early growth   ☐ Flowering   ☐ Fruiting   ☐ Going
to seed

HARVESTED? ☐ Yes   ☐ No

USED IN: _______________

NOTES:

My Field Notes

DATE: _________ **LOCATION:** ____________________________

PLANT NAME: _______________________________________

HABITAT + CONDITIONS:
☐ Prairie   ☐ Woodland edge   ☐ Wetland
☐ Roadside
☐ Dry   ☐ Moist   ☐ Sunny   ☐ Shady

OBSERVATIONS:
(leaves, flowers, scent, growth pattern)

____

____

____

STAGE:
☐ Early growth   ☐ Flowering   ☐ Fruiting   ☐ Going
to seed

HARVESTED? ☐ Yes   ☐ No

USED IN: _______________

NOTES:

My Field Notes

DATE: _________ **LOCATION:** _______________________

PLANT NAME: _______________________________

HABITAT + CONDITIONS:
☐ Prairie   ☐ Woodland edge   ☐ Wetland
☐ Roadside
☐ Dry   ☐ Moist   ☐ Sunny   ☐ Shady

OBSERVATIONS:
(leaves, flowers, scent, growth pattern)

____

____

____

STAGE:
☐ Early growth   ☐ Flowering   ☐ Fruiting   ☐ Going
to seed

HARVESTED? ☐ Yes   ☐ No

USED IN: _______________

NOTES:

My Field Notes

DATE: _________ **LOCATION:** _______________________________

PLANT NAME: ____

HABITAT + CONDITIONS:
☐ Prairie ☐ Woodland edge ☐ Wetland
☐ Roadside
☐ Dry ☐ Moist ☐ Sunny ☐ Shady

OBSERVATIONS:
(leaves, flowers, scent, growth pattern)

____

____

____

STAGE:
☐ Early growth ☐ Flowering ☐ Fruiting ☐ Going to seed

HARVESTED? ☐ Yes ☐ No

USED IN: _______________

NOTES:

My Field Notes

DATE: _________ **LOCATION:** _____________________________

PLANT NAME: _____________________________________

HABITAT + CONDITIONS:
☐ Prairie   ☐ Woodland edge   ☐ Wetland
☐ Roadside
☐ Dry   ☐ Moist   ☐ Sunny   ☐ Shady

OBSERVATIONS:
(leaves, flowers, scent, growth pattern)

____

____

____

STAGE:
☐ Early growth   ☐ Flowering   ☐ Fruiting   ☐ Going
to seed

HARVESTED? ☐ Yes   ☐ No

USED IN: _________________

NOTES:

About the Author

Sabrina Halvorson is a journalist by profession and a naturalist by heart. She is a Minnesota Master Naturalist and a coordinator for Herbalists Without Boarders in North Dakota.

Her 35-year career in journalism taught her to pay attention to the small details in the world around her. That same instinct now fuels her passion for wild plants and everything nature provides.

She studied plants and herbalism informally for decades while raising kids and creating a successful career. Once time allowed, she pursued a more formal education in botany and nature. She became a University of Minnesota Master Naturalist and graduated from the Chestnut School of Herbal Medicine, all while continuing her journalism career.

Sabrina lives in North Dakota with her husband, Rusty, and their cat, Rosie, whose favorite herb is catnip (obviously). Her two grown children, who live on opposite ends of the U.S., are her pride and joy. Find more of her work on foraging at thefumblingforager.com.